C000137644

1 MONTH OF
FREE
READING

at
www.ForgottenBooks.com

By purchasing this book you are eligible for one month membership to ForgottenBooks.com, giving you unlimited access to our entire collection of over 1,000,000 titles via our web site and mobile apps.

To claim your free month visit:
www.forgottenbooks.com/free1114544

ISBN 978-0-331-37855-9
PIBN 11114544

Historic, archived document

Do not assume content reflects current
scientific knowledge, policies, or practices.

WEEKLY STATION REPORTS

OF THE DIVISION OF

DRY LAND AGRICULTURE

BUREAU OF PLANT INDUSTRY

U. S. DEPARTMENT OF AGRICULTURE

GPO   123668

REPORT FOR THE WEEK ENDING JULY 2, 1938.

HAVRE:
Showery weather with ample precipitation characterized the week.
The total rainfall in June was 3.99 inches, and since May 1, 6.50
inches, as compared to a normal of 4.64 inches for these two months.
Precipitation having been well distributed, and temperatures moderate,
all crops are in excellent condition.
Harvesting various forages comprised the principal activity in
the experimental field. Cultivation of fallow was completed, and several
late dates of planting were made.
The first cutting of alfalfa has been started, rains and wet
ground hindering the curing process. Fallow in field C received its
first cultivation. Fences and bridges damaged by the recent flood
are being repaired.
Visitors included R. M. Williams, Superintendent of Judith
Basin Branch Station; and E. G. Davis of the U. S. Entomological
Laboratory, Bozeman.
Maximum temperature, 83°; minimum, 51°; precipitation, 1.28 inches.

JUDITH BASIN:
Cool weather with rain recorded every day during the week
has again made possible a good growth of crops. Although many
cloudbursts and flash rains have been reported in the area, only one
was received at the station. Friday afternoon a heavy rain with
some hail precipitated 0.85 inch in less than 30 minutes. There was
some hail injury in the plots, but this may be somewhat overcome as
the crops continue to mature. There was considerable run-off from
this flash rain.
Wet conditions this week have prevented the tillage of plots
and have halted haying operations a number of times. The early sweet-
clover varieties have been cut. Cattle were weighed, clipping tests
were made, and the listing of quadrats was completed in the pasture
trials. Hoeing and cultivation of shelterbelts has been continued.
Visitors were Mr. Wilkie Collins, Jr. and Mr. Fried of the
Soil Conservation Service, Rapid City, S. Dak.
Maximum temperature 76°; minimum, 47°; precipitation 1.61 inches.

HUNTLEY:
Favorable temperatures together with timely showers have
greatly benefited corn which has doubled its height during the last
week. Other crops have also made a marked growth, with winter wheat
and rye beginning to turn. Winter rye will need only a few more warm
days to bring it to maturity. A small, dashing shower caused some
lodging in barley and rye plots, but the condition is not yet serious.

This shower was the edge of a hail storm which swept a nearby community and resulted in heavy crop losses.

Spring pigs were moved from the winter rye to the field peas pasture during the week. Fall pigs were removed from alfalfa pastures to the dry lot for finishing. Forage produced this season has been very palatable, and the hogs have made good gains.

Precipitation for the three months, April-June amounted to 7.74 inches, or 147 percent of the average. The distribution and the manner in which the showers fell have been exceptionally good. Dashing showers have been few, and much of the precipitation has fallen as long, soaking rains. These were followed by windless, cloudy days and cool weather. Crops have outgrown weeds in the plots, but weeds have made a heavy growth in uncropped areas and continue to demand considerable labor for their control.

Maximum temperature 85°; minimum, 51°; precipitation, 0.26 inch.

SHERIDAN:

Continued frequent showers, light at the station but heavy in some nearby localities, delayed work with hay considerably. Much hay was about ready for the stack previous to the rain of last week, and only in the last day or so has it been dried out long enough to get much of it up. The most of the hay on the station had been gotten up in good shape with no rain on it, but some from roadways, bulk fields, and the rotation plots was out through the rain.

All crops continue to make good progress, with some winter rye and wheat now fairly well filled and beginning to turn. All lodged grain in the rotations straightened up well after drying off, but a considerable amount of barley and some winter wheat in other seedings are lodged quite badly. Corn made a rapid growth over the last two weeks, and, although planted late, the growth is now about average for the season. Thinning and the first cultivation of corn was completed.

Maximum temperature, 85°; minimum, 52°; precipitation, 0.15 inch.

DICKINSON:

Only light showers fell at the station during the week, but some nearby localities received much heavier amounts. June rainfall of 4.70 inches with moderate temperatures has resulted in a better crop outlook than in 1937 when the June precipitation amounted to 6.32 inches. Drought in 1937 continued until May 30, so that all creps were late in starting. Since the middle of May ample moisture and moderate temperatures have been favorable for the development of all crops.

Wheat is now nearly fully headed, tall, and leafy. Victory oats on the rotations are not yet fully headed. Barley is further advanced than either wheat or oats. Corn, millet, sorgo, and Sudan grass have made an excellent start. Even soybeans look promising, are now about 6 inches high, and, so far, have been grazed only a little by jackrabbits and blister beetles.

Sweet corn planted April 29 in a warm soil where sheltered by trees is about 3 feet high and beginning to tassel. Stands of corn at the station are generally good. In the district much damage was done by cutworms. Some replanting with sorgo and millet has been done.

Native grasses have made an excellent growth the past month. More grass has headed than for several years. Blue grama began heading during the week.

Trees and shrubbery have made a vigorous growth. Some trees which appeared early in the spring might fail to start have made an excellent growth. Nearly perfect stands have become established of blocks planted this spring to cedar, blue spruce, bull pine, ash, elm, and hackberry; Cedar and spruce 2 to $2\frac{1}{2}$ feet high, transplanted in April and May, have all made a good growth.

A moderate southeast wind today is bringing in a good many grasshoppers. This is the first movement on to the station this year. In 1936 they moved in on July 3 and in 1937 on July 6, after those which hatched on the station had been cleaned up by poison. In the southern part of this county and in Hettinger County much more damage was observed a week ago than in this locality.

Stem rust is increasing on wheat. Several days during the week were favorable for its development.

Maximum temperature, 83°; minimum, 47°; precipitation, 0.35 inch.

A rain of 1.37 inches accompanied by hail fell between 4:20 and 4:40 p.m. today(July 2). Run-off was excessive, washing across plots and roadways and carrying away more soil than any rain during recent years. Oats and barley on the rotations lodged worse than wheat. Corn and garden crops were badly riddled but will recover. Grains were not severely damaged by hail.

MANDAN:

Agronomy. - Frequent showers during the past week delayed haying operations. Some of the hay that was down got wet several times before it could be stacked.

Some cultivating of row crops was done, and the late fallow plots were plowed on July 1.

Crops have improved since the good rain of last week. Some of the fall-plowed grain plots were too far gone to recover.

Weeds are coming on rapidly over most of the fields. Rust is showing up in a number of plots. Weather has been favorable for its development during the past several days. Its spread depends entirely on weather conditions for the next few days. Temperatures have not been excessive, but the humidity has been high.

The total rainfall for June was 3.11 inches,with 2.76 inches of it during the last week. This is slightly below the average. The total for the year to date is 8.74 inches. This is slightly above the station average and below the long-time average.

Maximum temperature 84°, minimum, 48°; precipitation, 0.73 inch.

Cooperative Grazing Experiment: - The total rainfall at the pasture for June was 3.61 inches. Grass, especially blue grama, has improved greatly since the rains of last week. All pastures are furnishing plenty of feed at present. Blue grama grass is just starting to head out.

The steers were weighed at the end of June. Their gains were not as high as expected, nor as high as during June 1937. It may be that the drought during most of June held the grass back from its best growth.

The steers in the reserve pasture showed the highest gain, but their gain for the period in May was low.

The following table shows the steer gains for June and for the 40 days of pasture.

Pasture (Acres)	Steers (Number)	Gain perhead (lbs) June	40 days
100	10	49.5	99.5
70	10	46.5	97.0
50	10	51.5	94.0
30	10	62.0	100.5
70-rotation	14	44.6	94.3
7-crested wheat	4	47.5	100.0
12.5-mixed 1/	6	60.8	115.0
93-reserve	11	39.5	113.2
Average	75	56.8	100.9

The 50- and the 30-acre pastures were not grazed in 1937
1/All crested wheatgrass.

Arboriculture: - Cultivation and hoeing has continued on favorable days during the week. Dead wood has been removed from some of the testing blocks. A new pipe line has been laid in the conifer nursery.

Beetles and grasshoppers are continuing to do heavy damage to caragana and the few remaining elm seedlings.

A number of farm shelterbelts of varying ages have been visited in this immediate locality. The majority of them are in excellent condition.

Visitors for the week included J. Allen Clark, Wheat Investigations, Cereal Crops and Diseases; Dr. Ralph U. Cotter, Rust Survey, University Farm, St. Paul, Minn. F. G. Butcher, Entomology, N. Dak. Agricultural College; R. C. Newcomer, County Agent, Merton County, N. Dak., with 40 members of the 4H Club.

BELLE FOURCHE: Report for week ending June 25, 1938.

Injurious hot weather prevailed during the first half of the week, but the last 3 days were cooler, unsettled, and cloudy. Beneficial local rains occurred over much of the surrounding region, but only light showers were received at the station.

The hot weather materially increased the drought injury to all early crops. Some of the spring grain on fall plowing and spring plowing has burned beyond recovery without heading or attaining much growth. Small grain on fallow succeeded in fully heading and should produce fair yields if rains are received in the near future. Corn and potatoes made a vigorous growth during the warm weather. Sudan grass is up with only partial, uneven stands, owing to lack of moisture in the seed bed.

Grasshoppers present a very serious threat to all crops in the Belle Fourche Valley. In addition to the large number of young hoppers which hatched, and are still hatching, locally, the air is filled with migrating grasshoppers every day during fair weather. A large flight of grasshoppers apparently settled on the dry-land rotation field, early in the week, but fortunately the pests have not been feeding heavily during the recent cloudy, wet weather. It is doubtful if repeated distributions of poison bait under favorable conditions will be sufficiently effective to save crops.

Field work consisted mostly of hoeing and thinning corn and sorgo, hoeing alleys, and spraying potatoes.
Maximum temperature, 97°; minimum, 53°; precipitation 0.68 inch.

BELLE FOURCHE: Report for week ending July 2, 1938.
Warm weather prevailed throughout the week, and the drought continued unbroken. Only 0.92 inch precipitation, distributed in 10 light showers, was received during the month of June, as compared with the average for the month of 2.56 inches. The total precipitation from January to June, inclusive, was 6.28 inches, which is 2.35 inches less than the 30-year average for the 6-month period.

The warm, dry weather materially hastened the ripening of winter wheat, winter rye, and barley; and harvesting will commence 10 days to 2 weeks earlier than usual. Corn, potatoes, and sorgo continue to make a good growth. Some improvement in the stands of Sudan grass has occurred since the showers of the previous week, but considerable seed still remains in dry soil.

Grasshoppers are beginning to do serious damage to small grain, corn, and potatoes on rotation plots. Poison bait was distributed daily, and many of the pests were killed, but they were more than replaced by the influx of migrating grasshoppers. Flea beetles and blister beetles are also present in abnormally large numbers, and are doing considerable damage to potatoes, sugar beets, and garden creps throughout the Belle Fourche Valley.
Maximum temperature, 88°; minimum, 48°; precipitation, 0.07 inch.

ARCHER:
Cool weather prevailed during the fore part of the week, but the temperatures rose and the greater part of the week was warm. Local showers were common, but the station received none of consequence. The total precipitation for June was 1.96 inches, or 0.07 inch more than the 25-year average.

Crop prospects have improved generally. Spring wheat and oats are heading, and barley is fully headed. Corn, potatoes, millet, and beans have made good growth. Weeds have also responded to the moisture.

Station work consisted of weeding and hauling and stacking the rye hay.
John S. Cole; Director W. L. Quayle; J. Allen Clark; and H. F. Murphy, Experiment Station, Stillwater, Okla., were station visitors.
Maximum temperature, 83°; minimum, 49°; precipitation, 0.05 inch.

NORTH PLATTE:

The month of June closed with a moisture deficit of 0.96 inch. Only one rain fell during the month which was of much benefit to crops, all other showers were 0.25 inch or less. The month was comparatively cool with only one day with a temperature of 100°.

The rainfall for the first 6 months was 2.22 inches above normal. The excess moisture in April and May resulted in rank growth of grain, and there was little reservo moisture to carry the crops after the first of June. The drought period the first 3 weeks of the month caused rapid deterioration of the small grain, especially the winter wheat and oats. The barley looked good and gave premise of a good crop until strong warm winds the first 3 days of the week caused the grain to dry up rather than ripen normally. The grasshopper situation continues to be a serious problem. The hoppers are moving from the grain plots and grass into the corn, and several of the plots at the present have only 9 rows instead of the usual 10. Good kills have been gotten from frequent applications of poison, but there is apparently little reduction in the hopper population.

The corn was cultivated for the second time during the week, and harvest was started. The oats and barley in the D.L.A. plots have been harvested, and the winter wheat will be cut within the next few days.

A heavy rain with some hail fell at the station within a few minutes on Saturday evening. The amount of hail or rain falling at the dry land station was not reported at the time this report was written. The corn was quite badly stripped at the main buildings.

Visitors this week were John S. Cole, F. A. Coffman, and Mr. Atkinson of the Department of Agriculture in Australia.

Maximum temperature, 98; minimum, 55; precipitation, 0.10 inch.

AKRON:

The week was a continuation of the hot, dry weather with fewer local thunder showers. June closed with 1.15 inches of precipitation. This low precipitation has caused sharp premature ripening of a very promising small grain crop.

Rotation corn was cultivated for the first time. Harvesting was started on the rotations Thursday, and the most of the oats and barley are in shock. The binder was started in the cereal variety oats and barley Friday afternoon. Nursery harvesting was actively started Wednesday.

The hot weather has started active growth in the corn, millets, sorghums, and beans.

Eight hundred pounds of poison bait was scattered for the third consecutive week. There is a suspicion by this week end that grasshoppers are migrating in, and that this station may yet have a real fight to preserve the later seeded row crops. The boot webworm menace has abated, those not killed having attained full growth and gone down to pupate.

Annual small grains field day was held Tuesday through fine cooperative efforts of the Colorado State College. About 150 well filled cars from 14 Colorado counties taxed our facilities, but the day was weathered without too much confusion.

'Among other visitors were F. A. Coffman, Lindsay Brown, F. A. Hayes, E. W. Knoble, R. P. Yates, Wayne Austin, L. L. Zook, and John S. Cole.

Maximum temperature 99°; minimum, 49°; precipitation, Trace.

COLBY:

This week was fairly hot and dry with considerable dust and some soil blowing on two days. All small grains have ripened rapidly, and the row crops have made rapid growth. There may be better weather for ripening winter wheat, but judging from the wheat that has been combined so far, it does not appear that the quality has been hurt much. Most of the wheat that is coming to the elevators now is testing between 60 and 64 pounds. The yield is running from less than 10 to more than 25 bushels to the acre. Many fields where the straw is tall show much shriveling of the grain as harvest approaches, so that the quality will not be uniformly high. In the north half of the county where the wheat was hailed in May, it is safe to say that a big percentage of the wheat in this county will be of very high quality, probably the best in the State. The color is generally a dark, bright red, and the protein content is fairly high.

The wheat on the station is almost ready for combining. The plots to be harvested with a binder were cut yesterday. The straw is from 20 to 24 inches tall. The heads are short, and the grains are plump but not many to the head. Soil samples show that the first foot is not yet completely dry. The spring small grains are almost ripe.

Grasshoppers are very thick, in spite of almost daily poisoning. For a while it looked as though the poison was thinning them out, but the last few days they seem to be more numerous and hungrier than ever. They are damaging the corn plots very materially. The sorghums are up and appear to be getting well rooted.

Maximum temperature, 98°; minimum, 51°; precipitation, 0.01 inch.

Precipitation for June, 2.61 inches.

HAYS:

The week has been hot. Temperatures have ranged between 52° and 106°.

Winter wheat is now dead ripe on all the plots and all over the county. It did not really ripen, it just dried up. The earliest wheat, however, was far enough along that some of it is turning out good yields of good quality. On the other hand many fields, and all the later wheat fields, are making low yields of poor quality. There was none of the golden color to be seen at any time below the heads of wheat that matures normally.

Combines are now humming in all fields. On the project combine harvesting was commenced June 30, but was interrupted awaiting repairs for the tractor.

Hand harvesting of 1/1000 acre samples is in progress from certain

plots on which a study is being made of yields from individual rows
of wheat that was drilled on sorghum land.

Spring wheat was harvested with a binder today. It was not fully
matured but was almost dried up, and the grasshoppers were cutting off
many of the heads. The grasshoppers were trimming off the beards in
such a way that much of the wheat looked like a beardless wheat.

Thinning of sorghum plots has been completed. Partial thinning
of corn has also been completed. Because of the threat of grasshopper
injury to the corn, it was left a little thicker than is desired for a
permanent stand. More plants will be removed later if necessary after
we find how much the grasshoppers devour. They are eating into the
fleshy part of the stalks cutting some of them off near the ground, or
cutting so deep into the plant that it falls over at the weakened point.
In many instances their work looks like that of rabbits.

A large amount of grasshopper poison was spread during the week.
The grasshoppers appear to be coming into the plots now from adjoining
field and take a few good feeds on the corn before they can be killed
with poison.

Maximum temperature, 106°; minimum, 52°; precipitation, 0.

GARDEN CITY:

The total rainfall for June was 1.32 inches, normal is 2.71 inches.
The total for the 6 months, January-June was 7.46 inches, normal for the
same period is 8.76 inches. Dust occurred on one day this week, making
a total of seven dusty days for June as compared with five for the same
month last year.

Field work consisted of lightly one-waying the wheat plots to destroy
the thistles and stop moisture loss. Various implements were used on the
basin lister project to prepare the plots for fallow, namely the 44-inch
and the 20-inch basin listers, ordinary lister, one-way, and the one-way
basin attachment.

Row crops are making rapid growth but will be in need of moisture
in the near future, especially those on continuous cropped land.

Maximum temperature, 103°; minimum, 60°; precipitation, T.

TUCUMCARI:

Row crops, although small and late, have shown the need for water
the past few days, with rising temperatures and brisk winds prevailing.
No cultivation has been performed, but thinning has begun. Cultivation
next week will be begun on those plots which have been thinned. Ranges
have lost their fresh appearance the past few days, showing the depletion
of near-surface moisture.

Variety wheat plots were threshed, the July 1 planting of forage
sorghums was made, and blow sand was moved from sand fences protecting
the station from neighboring fields.

Maximum temperature, 99°; minimum, 58°; precipitation, 0.12 inch.
June precipitation, 1.49 inches, precipitation January-June, 6.41 inche

O. R. Mathe visited the station yesterday, leaving today for
Dalhart.

DALHART:

The rotation kafir and milo plots will show stands except for
some of the listed plots and a few of the late worked plots. Cowpeas

and forage crops planted this week in nearly dry soil will show only
spotted emergence. Some increase Sudan was also planted this week, but
emergence was hardly expected on much of it. There was no rain during
the week.

Some increase fields of Finney milo were thinned this week, as
the plants were much too thick. Some seedling counts of Sedan kafir
for coleoptile color were made.

Maximum temperature for the week was 98^0; minimum, 59^0; precipitation, T.

The precipitation for the first 6 months was 4.36 inches, and for
the 12 months ending June 30 was 10.00 inches. The precipitation for
the first half of 1938 is approximately 50 percent of normal.

BIG SPRING:

A slow rain which started last week continued over Saturday and
Sunday with a total of 0.99 inch for the week. During the month of
June rains varying from 0.05 to 2.28 inches were recorded on 11 days.
The total for the month is 6.85 inches, as compared with a normal of
2.17, and for the first 6 months of the year it is 13.60 inches as
compared with 8.91 inches, the average. Since 1900 there has been
only one year, 1919, when the June rainfall exceeded that received
during the past month.

Ideal growing conditions prevailed during the past week, with the
result that all crops although late are now making a rapid growth.
Thinning of sorghums and knifing have occupied the major portion of the
time of the station force during the week. All milo, kafir, corn,
broomcorn, and sumac sorgo in the rotations have been thinned and the
entire field knifed over.

O. R. Mathews of the Dry Land Office and Bradford Knapp Jr. of
the Animal Husbandry Division visited the station during the week.

Maximum temperature for the week, 93^0; minimum, 64^0; precipitation, 0.99
inch.

LAWTON:

The vigorous growth of row crops and the higher maximum temperatures of the past week rapidly dissipated the rainfall of 1.12 inches
received on the 25th. All row crops were cultivated during the week.
In the grain sorghum variety test several early maturing sorghums are
showing the first heads. Some of the kafir plots in the rotations will
be heading in the near future. Feterita is very irregular in growth and
shows rather heavy chinch-bug injury.

Threshing of rotation wheat plots and the spring seedings of oats
was begun July 1. The quality of the grain in each case is poor, and
the yields will be rather low. Threshing of wheat and oats throughout
the county is now in full swing. Yields are low and the quality of the
grain is poor. The June rainfall of 3.20 inches brought the 6-month
total up to 21.66 inches - 6.62 inches above normal. It was the general
impression that June was a rather cool month, but the mean monthly
temperature was 0.6^0 above normal.

WOODWARD:

The week ended with a total of 0.07 inch of precipitation. This was divided into two small showers for the fore part of the week. Warm weather for the latter part of the week was accompanied by a brisk wind from the southwest, the result being warm wind.

Corn has begun tasseling. Quite a variation in height of corn is apparent among the various plots. M.C. plots A and C are approximately the same height and are taller than plot B. All sorghums with the exception of replanted plots were thinned, and cultivation will be completed today (Saturday). Replanted sorghums and cowpeas have emerged to a fair stand. Replanted cowpeas were very small to be cultivated, but the cultivation was to stop the sifting in of sand. Bound rye and wheat were thrashed but have not been cleaned and weighed. Apparently the rye yields for this season are higher than the average.

Fallow plots and roadways on the west place were cultivated to stop sifting of dust.

Harvesting, thinning and cultivating sorghums, replacing straw on rye plots, mulching contour trees and shrubbery with straw, and cutting and storing alfalfa hay constituted the work for the week.

Station visitors were O. R. Mathews, A. L. Hallsted, and C. R. Enlow.

Maximum temperature, 101°; minimum, 60°; precipitation, 0.07 inch.

WEEKLY STATION REPORTS

OF THE DIVISION OF

DRY LAND AGRICULTURE

BUREAU OF PLANT INDUSTRY

U. S. DEPARTMENT OF AGRICULTURE

GPO   123668

REPORT FOR THE WEEK ENDING JULY 9, 1938.

HAVRE:

Frequent showers occurred. Since May 1 precipitation has totaled 7.68 inches, rainfall being recorded on 41 of the 70 days. Temperatures have been about normal, with no high maxima. Under such conditions range land and crops are the best in at least a decade. Summer fallowed land is wet through the third foot.

Haying in the agronomy field continued when weather permitted. Second-year alfalfa in rotation 42 produced 3,640 pounds of hay per acre. Winter rye for hay on fallow yielded over 3 tons of field cured forage. Some poisoning to control grasshoppers has become necessary in various projects. Says plant bug is reported in damaging numbers nearby, the infestation on the station until the present time being slight.

The farm department has been engaged in putting up a large yield of first cutting alfalfa hay, operations having been hindered greatly by rain. To date actual spoilage was avoided, however, all of the hay stacked thus far is discolored. Winter rye for hay in field C was harvested early in the week, and an increase seed tract is now being bound.

Owing to the June flood, all livestock fences in the Beaver Creek basin were badly wrecked, and a W.P.A. emergency relief crew of 10 men is engaged in salvaging and repairing the damage. Grass at the Bear Paw lease has made excellent growth, and the breeding herds appear in good condition.

Maximum temperature, 87°; minimum, 53°; precipitation, 0.34 inch.

JUDITH BASIN:

Continued rains during the week have brought the precipitation to date to above normal for the year. Thursday broke a 16-day total of consecutive days of precipitation. Wet weather has delayed and hindered haying operations as well as the cutting of forage grasses for hay.

Tillage of some rotation plots has again been started. Some hoeing and cultivation has been done in the shelterbelts and corn plots this week. Taking notes and cutting of the forage plots has finally begun.

Maximum temperature, 81°; minimum, 46°; precipitation, 1.35 inches.

HUNTLEY:

Good growing temperatures together with almost daily showers have been beneficial to all crops during the week. Corn, beans, and sorgos continue to grow rapidly, and grain crops appear to be developing nicely. Winter wheat has all turned color on the side of maturity, and, although there are lodged spots in some of the plots, ripening is quite uniform. There is also some lodging in the heavier barley plots. Weeds have made a heavy growth during the period when the soil was too wet to cultivate, and considerable hand weeding and hoeing will be necessary before the fields are again cleaned up.

Field work has consisted of cultivating row crops, hauling in late-cut hay, soil sampling, and hoeing weeds.

Maximum temperature, 90°; minimum, 46°; precipitation, 0.80 inch.

SHERIDAN:

With temperatures continuing slightly below the average for the season, and one heavy shower over the main part of the station, crops generally continued to make good progress. Weeds also are growing fast, rough pigweed having made a heavy growth in the flax varieties over the past two weeks, even with a fair stand and growth of the flax. Much of the early barley and winter wheat are ripening fast, and some harvesting probably will be necessary next week. The first cultivation of all annual row crops was completed, and the most of the grain that can be saved for seed purposes was rogued. Second growth of early cut alfalfa is in bloom, with about as heavy a growth as for the first cutting.

Considerable damage by grasshoppers has been noted this week, and poison bait is being spread today.

Maximum temperature, 89°; minimum, 49°; precipitation, 0.99 inch.

DICKINSON:

Development of crops was rapid during the week. Grains are filling, and early seeded fields are in the milk to soft dough stage of development. Early barley is somewhat further along. It appears that two weeks will be required for maturity. Rust has developed rapidly, and promises to be the most severe of recent years. In fact the race is now between rust and grasshoppers. Yesterday grasshoppers in great numbers moved in covering everything. They have started work on all crops but are thickest on barley and oats. Most of the beards are being cut from the barley, some of the stems and grains cut off, and the kernels eaten. Many of the kernels are being cut from oats. These grains are still too immature to make a high quality of feed if cut. The grasshoppers are numerous in grass plots and everywhere about the place. Unless these hoppers move on shortly, it appears most of a very promising crop will be lost.

Corn and garden crops as well as grains have recovered rapidly from the hail and torrential rain of July 2.

Visitors included H. B. Elmendorf, hydraulic engineer, Bureau of Agricultural Economics; S. H. Hastings and Dan Hansen, Western Irrigation Agriculture; Geo. Baker, Director of Extension; and Gray Butcher, Extension Entomologist.

Maximum temperature, 82°; minimum, 54°; precipitation, 2.25 inches.

MANDAN:

Agronomy - More rain fell during the week. On the morning of the 4th, 0.54 inch was recorded and 0.63 on the 5th. The soil is well soaked at present. There was little run-off.

Weeds are making a rapid growth. Corn was given the second cultivation.

All crops have improved since the recent rains. Corn is exceptionally good. Wheat has improved on all plots, except some fall plowed that were burned beyond recovery. Rust increased on wheat, and the infection is now serious.

Maximum temperature, 89°; minimum, 59°; precipitation, 1.18 inches.

Cooperative Grazing Experiment - Pastures have improved greatly since the rains. Blue grama grass has made a rapid growth, and is now furnishing an abundance of feed. It is fully headed out on many spots over the prairie.

Horticulture - The third and last spray of the season has been applied. Arsenate of lead, nicotine sulphate, and fish oil soap were the ingredients used. Aphids were bad on some of the plums and leafhoppers on the grapes.

Juneberries, red currants, and part of the Chinese cherries have been picked. The Juneberry crop was heavy, but the other two were light. Seedlings of Success Juneberry in the breeding blocks do not show as much variation as one might expect, but resemble the parent to a marked degree. Gooseberries are ripening, and two new selections have been made. We also have made a few new selections of the Nanking or Chinese cherry, one of which seems to be very good.

Garden vegetables are yielding well and making a good growth since the recent rains.

Arboriculture - E. J. George writes from Parshall, N. Dak., on July 6: "Grain crops generally good although some fields apparently burned before rain came. Very little grasshopper injury at present; small amount of stem rust. Trees generally good; 1938 plantings practically 100 percent stand. Rain soaked down to 3 feet and below." He will be traveling through Montana for the remainder of the month inspecting shelterbelt plantings.

Visitors for the week included Leroy Moomaw, Superintendent, Dickinson Substation; S. H. Hastings and Dan Hansen, Western Irrigation Agriculture; Nat. C. Murray, formerly in charge of Division of Crop Estimates; and R. B. Jadcard, Minneapolis Grain Corporation.

ARCHER:

The weather during the week ending July 9 was warm and dry with a cool spell during July 6. Three local showers, totalling 0.29 inch of precipitation, occurred. Nineteen days have passed since the station received a substantial amount of precipitation. The crops and pastures are in need of moisture, but no serious damage has resulted, except that the native grasses have taken on a gray-green appearance and the leaves have started to roll.

During the week the larger fields of corn and fallow were cultivated, the peas for green manure were plowed under, and the clover plots were cut. The second cultivation of the alleyways and the corn and potato plots will be practically finished today. The hoeing of these plots is also nearing completion.

Maximum temperature, 88°; minimum, 42°; precipitation, 0.29 inch.

NORTH PLATTE:

Two heavy rains fell during the week. From the first, which fell Saturday night and was accompanied by considerable hail at the main buildings, 0.68 inch was recorded at the dry land station and 1.05 inches on the bench. The second was on Wednesday evening. Before this rain, a dust storm limited visibility to about 100 yards, and a heavy wind accompanied the rain which followed the dust. 1.35 inches with some hail fell in less than an hour, and some damage was done to the corn and sorghums. The two rains were of such a nature that there was a large percentage of run-off.

The binding of the plots and varieties was completed during the week, and threshing will follow in a few days.

G. A. Wiebe visited the station during the week.

Maximum temperature, 100°; minimum, 53°; precipitation, 2.30 inches.

AKRON:

Harvesting full blast with two binders and a nursery crew did not enable the station to keep fully abreast of the forced ripening of the small grains. The most of the rate and date, and the rotation winter wheat plots remain. By the time these are harvested, the spring wheat promises to be dead ripe. The uniformly cropped plots to the west now appears as a thickly shocked field. They ran rather uniformly 72 to 80 bundles per tenth-acre plot.

The late spring planted crops in rows and in drill seedings look very promising, with corn standing about knee high. The lack of rainfall has minimized the weed problem on these plots. Grasshoppers continue to become increasingly menacing. A mechanical bait spreader has been acquired to aid in the fight against these pests, which are concentrating in the green plots as the small grain harvest progresses.

G. A. Wiebe arrived Friday and was met here by J. J. Curtis and Warren Leonard from Fort Collins. Mr. Wiebe's chief interest was the barley plantings. Mr. Leonard made a thorough inspection of the corn plantings.

Maximum temperature, 95°; minimum, 50°; precipitation, 0.23 inch.

COLBY:

Almost ideal harvest weather has prevailed nearly all week. A shower of nearly a half-inch delayed combining for half of the day Thursday. The first four days of the week the temperatures rose to above 100°, but during the last 3 days they were much lower.

The D.L.A. plots were harvested with the combine on Tuesday, Wednesday, and Thursday. The straw was generally short and there were no weeds, so that the combining proceeded without any delays. The quality of the winter wheat is uniformly high. It has a very bright color, appearing as though it would be rather high in protein. The test weight on some of the highest yielding plots ranged around 63 pounds. Plot M.F. 2 A, fallowed entirely with the oneway, which yielded 13.8 bushels to the acre, was the highest yielding plot. The other fallow plots in the same series averaged

from 7.2 on the June plowing without previous tillage, to 12.3
bushels on the plot worked entirely with the duckfoot. Plots
M.C.A,B, and C yielded 5.3, 4.7, and 5.2, respectively. In
rotations 551 to 560, the plot in 554 which receives a top
dressing of straw was distinctly the poorest, those top dressed
with manure were next, and those which never receive any manure
were the best. Plot 553 A ranked second of all the plots with
a yield of 13.5 bushels. In rotation 155, not manured, the
wheat yielded 8.0 bushels, whereas in rotation 156, manured,
the yield was 5.7 bushels. In the soil conservation series
added last year the three plots with levees around them yielded
5.5, 4.8, and 5.0 bushels; those worked with a lister yielded
5.8 and 6.2 bushels; and those worked with the damming lister
yielded 5.8 and 6.0 bushels. Not much difference was expected
in the listing methods as they had no opportunity to catch
much water before they were worked down for seeding, but those
with levees caught the heavy rains of May and June. The lowest
yielding plot was 571 A, continuously stubbled in, which yielded
only 0.3 bushel, as little barley grass had choked out nearly all of
the wheat. The next lowest yield was 3.0 bushels on the stubbled
in plot in rotation 574. The two plots on three-year fallow
yielded 10.7 and 11.2 bushels. The winter wheat plots averaged
6.9 bushels, 9.6 on fallow and 5.9 on crop land. The spring
wheat yields ranged from 3.3 to 6.0 bushels and averaged 4.4
bushels. The spring wheat was somewhat shriveled. The barley
yields ranged from 2.1 to 7.1 bushels. The barley was shriveled
and very poor in every respect. It seems to have been a poor
year for Flynn. The yields of oats ranged from 7.2 to 8.8 bushels.
The grain was rather light for Kanota oats. The plots which were
most promising a month earlier did not finish quite so well
as the less promising ones.

Corn and sorghums are making fairly rapid growth. The
half inch shower seemed to freshen things up considerably.
Grasshoppers have caused many of the corn plants to fall over,
injuring the stands very materially on some of the plots. They
continued very numerous up to a few days ago in spite of heavy
mortality from poisoning. Most of them seem to have left,
however, during the last three days.

John S. Cole and A. L. Hallsted visited the station
Tuesday, and O. R. Mathews and Lindsey Brown were here Thursday.
Maximum temperature, 104°; minimum, 55°; precipitation, 0.54 inch.

HAYS:

Weather during the week has been for the most part clear
and hot interrupted by short intervals of part cloudiness and
two showers too small to be of value to growing crops, but large
enough to interfere with combine harvesting two half days.

Corn, kafir, and mile crops are making good growth;
but corn is suffering severely from grasshoppers, despite the
fact large amounts of poison bait have been spread repeatedly.

Combine harvesting has been going very satisfactorily, although a little slow owing to the fact that the straw is badly lodged which makes it necessary to cut low and handle large amounts of straw. The largest number of plots harvested in a single day this year is 76. If nothing interferes the harvest will be almost finished today.

Visitors during the past two weeks have been many. Among those were President Farrell and Dean Call of the Kansas State College, and J. S. Cole.

Maximum temperature, 109°; minimum, 57°; precipitation, 0.10 inch.

GARDEN CITY:

Only 0.01 inch and one trace of moisture was recorded this week. Except for this and a trace, no moisture has fallen since June 24. During this period were 7 consecutive days of 100° temperatures or more. The drilled Sudan grass and flax are beginning to burn, and a few of the row crops are wilting.

Field work consisted of cultivating row crops, hoeing weeds, and taking soil moisture samples on milo plots.

Station visitors were President F. D. Farrell, Director L. E. Call and Dr. Lamour, of the Kansas State College; O. R. Mathews; C. W. Brittain, Dry Land Agent at Woodward, Okla., Dr. L. A. Brown, Agronomist (Soils), Fort Collins, Colo., and H. T. U. Smith, Geologist, Lawrence, Kans.

Maximum temperature, 105°; minimum, 60°; precipitation, 0.01 inch.

TUCUMCARI:

With temperatures the highest of the year and with periods of hot, drying winds, ranges and young row crops have suffered acutely the past week. Since the close of May only 1.49 inches precipitation has been received, on 13 days, and the surface soil is very dry.

The late cowpea test, grain sorghum varieties, and Sudan grass on increase land were planted with surface planter run deep, but full stands may not emerge until after rain.

Thinning of plots is progressing rapidly, with the cultivator following thinning. Conifers planted this season were hoed and watered in the attempt to carry the young plants through this severe period.

Maximum temperature, 100°; minimum, 63°; precipitation, Trace.

DALHART:

Another dry week. Work during the week included the cultivation of some early seeded plots which were showing weedy. The chief weeds were the ubiquitous 'goatheads'. It was extremely difficult to see the dry soil further pulverized by the cultivations, but the weeds had to be removed. Some tree plantings were also worked. The thinning of row crops continued as did sand removal from the farmstead.

The earlier planted crops show good color and fair growth, although wilting of the sorghum plants is apparent. The later seeded sorghums are small. Some of these apparently will grow, but some of the plots have insufficient moisture in the surface soil to keep the seedlings alive very long. Wherever a thin layer of drift sand covered the seed the emergences were good. Cowpeas and late seeded forage plots show only a few plants.

Maximum temperature, 99°; minimum, 62°; precipitation, none.

BIG SPRING:

Ample soil moisture together with hot weather are two factors which have caused all crops to make a rapid growth during the past week. Late planted cotton and sorghums are just showing above the lister beds. All farmers have finally obtained good stands of cotton, but the important question with them now is, "Will it have time to mature before frost?".

Station work has consisted entirely of thinning cotton and sorghums and cultivating them. With the exception of a few plots of cotton planted July 1, all plot thinning was completed today. The rotations and all cooperative plots were also cultivated during the week.

Maximum temperature, 101°; minimum, 69°; precipitation, none.

LAWTON:

Maximum temperatures of 100° to 102° on five consecutive days the past week were too high for such sorghums as kafir and feterita that are rapidly breaking out of the boot.

One of the worst dust storms experienced this year occurred on the evening of the 7th, when a high wind from the northwest reduced visibility nearly to the zero point for about an hour. Crops suffered minor damage by broken stalks. A shower of 0.16 inch and a drop in temperature from 102° to 67° followed the storm and afforded considerable relief.

Threshing was completed during the week, and some tillage was performed on stubble land. About 15 acres of volunteer oats that was pastured through the winter and late spring, and injured by hail in May yielded approximately 12 bushels per acre of grain of good quality.

WOODWARD:

The fore part of the week was dry, hot, and windy. The spell was broken by a rain Wednesday night and Thursday. Temperature jumped up to 101° and 102° for five days continuously.

Plowing, one-waying, disking, listing, duckfooting, and basin listing plots after harvest in preparation for fallows and seedbeds for 1939 crops were completed today.

Station visitors for the week were: O.R.Mathews;H.A.Daniels, Supt.SCS sta.,Guthrie,Okla.;H.M.Elwell,Guthrie;R.D.Ferris,Nat'l.Park Service,Little Rock,Ark.;J.W.Farrent,Engineer,State Planning Board, Okla.City;D.C.Mooring,Extension Horti.,and F.K.McGinnis,Asst.Extension Horti.,Stillwater;E.R.Daniel,Asst.Extension Engineer,Stillwater; and Leroy Powers, Sr.Geneticist, Field Sta.,Cheyenne, Wyo.

Maximum temperature, 102°; minimum, 66°; precipitation, 0.90 inch.

NEWELL:

High temperatures, hot winds, and excessive evaporation during the fore part of the week were injurious to all early crops. Some relief was afforded by two days of cool, cloudy, unsettled weather which followed, but it was hot and windy again at the end of the week. Heavy rains occurred in nearby localities, but only a few light showers were received at the station.

Small grains are ripening very rapidly, and harvesting of winter rye, winter wheat, and barley was commenced. Corn and sorgo made normal growth, but corn began to curl badly during the last 2 days. Development of potatoes was checked by grasshoppers which are doing extensive damage to potato vines. Grasshoppers are injuring all crops except sorgo, but the damage to oats is more severe than to any of the other small grains.

Maximum temperature, 100°; minimum, 55°; precipitation, 0.28 inch.

-ooOoo-

WEEKLY STATION REPORTS

OF THE DIVISION OF

DRY LAND AGRICULTURE

BUREAU OF PLANT INDUSTRY

U. S. DEPARTMENT OF AGRICULTURE

GPO   123668

REPORT FOR THE WEEK ENDING JULY 16, 1938.

HAVRE:
        The weather during the week was clear and moderately warm, no
precipitation occurring.
        Early oats and barley are beginning to turn. Winter wheat is
also starting to ripen. The second cultivation of corn has been
completed, and the harvest of grass and alfalfa finished. Corn
breeding work was begun. Infestation of Says plant bug and
grasshoppers from nearby vacated farm land has rapidly increased
in the experimental field.
        Haying operations on the general farm were uninterrupted,
most of the first cutting alfalfa now being stacked. Reconstruction
of the livestock corrals and hay shed by W.P.A. is nearing completion.
    Maximum temperature, 92°; minimum, 52°; precipitation, none.

JUDITH BASIN:
        This week was the first without precipitation since the last
of May. The total precipitation for the year is now 10.10 inches.
The dry weather has permitted the cutting, weighing, and hauling of
forage plots and cutting of bulk fields for hay.
        Crops as a whole are in the best of condition, although
another good rain would be a decided aid to spring grains and corn.
To date there is no border effect on plots, a condition seldom seen
in dry land experiments at this stage of maturity.
        Besides haying operations, other work has consisted of culti-
vation of corn, tillage of rotation fallow plots and bulk fields,
and getting the grounds ready for the 29th annual picnic which will
be held Thursday, July 21.
        Visitors of the week include, Harold Tower, Soil Conservation
Service, Wash., D. C.; Ralph Tower, Polson, Mont.; M.P.Hansmeier,
State Soil Conservationist, Bozeman; and County Agents, E.R.Cook,
Big Timber; K. P. Jones, Harlowton; and Harold Dusenberry, Stanford.
    Maximum temperature, 85°; minimum, 49°; precipitation, none.

HUNTLEY:
        Fairly high temperatures and light precipitation during the
week have hastened the maturity of oats and barley on the plots,
but spring wheat is still green and making new growth. Most of the
winter wheat plots are about ready for the binder, although some
have small areas in them that are still a little green. Corn and
other late-sown crops, as well as the second crop alfalfa, have
made a good growth.

A heavy cover of downy bromegrass on the range and other uncultivated areas has matured to the stage at which it constitutes a serious fire hazard. Several large grass fires have occurred near the station during the week, but no damage to crops or livestock has been reported. Most of the wheat fields are protected by wide fire guards, but these do not always check the blaze when the wind is blowing.

Field work has consisted of weeding operations, harvesting grain hays, and plowing under late green manure crops.

Maximum temperature, 94°; minimum, 50°; precipitation, trace.

SHERIDAN:

Warm weather over the week was favorable for a rapid growth of corn and all late crops, including weeds. Grain ripened rapidly. Bulk rye, and winter wheat and Sparton barley in Field I, as well as early sown Trebi barley in the same field, were harvested, the 16 acres using an average of 4 pounds of twine per acre. Harvesting of one series of the rates of seeding barley which ripened ahead of the remainder was stopped this morning by heavy rain, which fell after any readings included in this report. Other work during the week consisted largely in cleaning up weeds where they were the worst, in some of the shelterbelts and in rotation alleys where they would cause trouble in harvesting, mowing alfalfa where second growth was sufficiently heavy, mowing rotation roads, second cultivation of corn and other row crops, and cultivation of fallow.

W. L. Quayle was at the station on the 12th.

Maximum temperature, 95°; minimum, 47°; precipitation, trace.

DICKINSON:

The heaviest migration of grasshoppers since the station was established moved into the district on Sunday, July 10, lesser movements having occurred both before and since. The number of hoppers still working seems to be at its maximum. Damage has been severe to all grain crops, with the greatest amount on barley and oats.

Oats and barley on the rotations were cut July 13 and 14 while still immature to try to get some measure of yield and to save part of the crop for feed. Oats were in the milk to dough stage of maturity, and barley was in the stiff dough stage. Hoppers had eaten nearly all the leaves and cut off from 10 to 50 percent of the oat kernels. They had clipped the beards from the barley and eaten some of the grain besides cutting off many of the heads. Oats, barley, and rye in the cereal project were cut July 15. Most of the oats and barley in the locality have been cut for feed.

On the Normal School field wheat plots were also severely damaged after the oats were cut. So far, corn, sorgo, and millet have been damaged but little, except sweet corn in the garden where considerable damage was done to the leaves and the silk.

Some damage is being done to trees and shrubbery. Most of the foliage has been eaten from the Russian olive hedge near the buildings and from caragana and Russian olive in the west shelter belt.

Fruit trees were sprayed, and the spray material seems to be acting to some extent as a repellant. Flowers and vegetables including potatoes have been dusted frequently trying to save them.

Rust continues to develop on grains. Since the leaves have nearly all been eaten by hoppers, and the remaining leaves, sheaths, and stems are heavily infested with rust, the grain is developing slowly with the indication that most of the wheat which survives the hoppers will be light in weight and yield.

Visitors included William Leary, Extension Agronomist; W. P. Sebens, State Seed Department; R. A. Kinzer, State Board of Administration; Paul Kasson, County Agent, Bowman; Vernon Thompson, County Agent, Medora; J. Allen Clark, Cereal Crops and Diseases; and Mr. Webber and R. P. Dougherty, Soil Conservation Service.

Maximum temperature, 87°; minimum, 43°; precipitation, 0.17 inch.

MANDAN:

Agronomy - The past week was favorable for all field work. Corn was given the second cultivation. Fallow was duckfooted.

Weeds have come on with a heavy growth after the rains. Pigeon grass and old witch grass are especially bad and have been mowed in the south field and field P.

Some bromegrass has been harvested for seed, and harvest of crested wheatgrass started today.

All grains are looking good. Grasshoppers are thick, but damage to date has not been severe. Rust shows a heavy infestation on some varieties. Kubanka on the plots shows some rust, but damage is not expected to be severe.

Maximum temperature, 91°; minimum, 50°; precipitation, 0.27 inch.

Cooperative Grazing Experiment - Native vegetation is in the best condition for grazing that it has been for a number of years. The first division of the rotation pasture was grazed for 55 days and still contains plenty of feed.

Blue grama grass is fully headed over the prairie. It has made a remarkable recovery from the droughts of 1934 and 1936.

While the grass is in excellent condition for grazing, the cattle are not doing as well as during some other years. The flies are exceptionally bad, and the cattle spend a great deal of time fighting them. Mosquitoes have appeared in vast numbers during the past few days.

Horticulture - Weeds, especially purslane, have been growing rapidly, encouraged by the recent rains and warm weather. Cultivation with teams and tractor and hoeing have been in progress throughout the week.

Golden currants are now ripening. Some of the selections are of large size and appear very promising.

Vegetables are growing apace, and a liberal assortment is harvested each day. A list of crops is given as follows: peas, wax and string beans, cabbage, cauliflower, beets, turnips, kohl rabi, onions, and New Zealand spinach.

Weeds are very abundant, and cultivating and hoeing has been in progress during the week. The fight against insect pests such as blister beetles, cabbage worms, and grasshoppers goes on daily, and so far they have not caused much damage to garden crops.

Cannas are coming into bloom and geraniums are picking up nicely. Hemerocallis in variety, Gaillardia, Platycodon, and Gypsophila are brightening the perennial borders.

Arboriculture - E. J. George reports as follows during the week from the several points visited:

July 8. Bowbells, N. Dak. - Crops continue good. Heavy grasshopper infestation in Kenmare vicinity. Heavy rains have fallen all over this vicinity. Trees good except those planted 5 years ago, which are mostly failures.

July 8. Williston, N. Dak. - Fair to good crops on most farms. Lakes frequent over the prairie, and much pasture land is now red with grama grass in head. Western wheatgrass also abundant on land which last year appeared devoid of any grass roots. Heavy rain at Crosby and west last night.

July 11. Plentywood, Mont. - Crops generally good everywhere and pastures coming back fast. With the small amount of stock now present grass should seed in well this year. Five-year old cooperative tree plantings continue to be poor, but all others are good.

July 13. Glasgow, Mont. Crops good in Opheim and Scoby country. Grasshoppers moving in this week and commencing to cause damage, particularly to rye. Some hail damage up to 20 percent Monday night. Every bridge and culvert out in some sections making travel hazardous.

July 14. Malta, Mont. - Grasshoppers moving in in swarms today. Livestock, few in number, are in excellent condition.

Visitors for the week included A. C. Dillman, Seed flax investigations; J. A. Munro, State Entomologist, N. Dak. Agric. College; L. D. Colidge, Economics, Columbia University.

Dept. of Interior, Porcupine Substation, tour of 40 Indians more particularly interested in fruit and vegetable growing.

Extension Conservationists, County Agents, and Agricultural Conservation Committeemen from nine Counties - Kidder, Logan, Emmons, Burleigh, Morton, Oliver, Sioux, Mercer, and McLean. Inspected grazing trials, old and new crested wheatgrass plantings, grass nurseries, and field and pasture terraces.

BELLE FOURCHE:

The week was a continuation of warm, dry weather, but the last day was cool and cloudy with occasional light drizzling showers. No precipitation of value to vegetation has been received since May 31, and all crops seeded prior to that date have been injured by the drought. Sudan grass and sorgo are making a normal growth, but corn is suffering seriously from lack of moisture, and grasshoppers are doing extensive damage to the crop. Potatoes were sprayed the third time to control blister beetles and other insects, but grasshoppers are gradually destroying the vines. Small grains have ripened rapidly, and only a few plots of spring wheat remain to be harvested on the dry land rotation field.

The annual picnic was held at the station on July 16, and the attendance was only slightly below normal, although the weather was unsettled and stormy. Principal speakers for the occasion were Congressman Francis Case, and State Secretary of Agriculture Gordon Stout.

Maximum temperature, 95°; minimum, 50°; precipitation, 0.12 inch.

ARCHER:

The weather during the week ending July 16 was quite warm. Two showers totaling 0.42 inch of precipitation occurred during the latter part of the week.

Crops on land in which there was no reserve soil moisture burned. Winter wheat and barley began to ripen. Corn rolled badly for a couple of days. The showers gave relief to crops.

All hay, except millet, was hauled from the rotation plots and weighed and stored... Practically all hay on increase areas was hauled. The greater portion of the Ceres wheat in the dairy field is being cut for hay. Weed work occupied the major portion of the station activities.

Dr. G. A. Weibe, Cereal Crops and Diseases, visited July 15.

Maximum temperature, 95°; minimum, 51°; precipitation, 0.42 inch.

NORTH PLATTE:

The weather for the week was quite variable. A heavy wind during Sunday night caused considerable soil movement, and it was necessary to reset several shocks on the D.L.A. plots. Temperatures of over 100° were recorded on two days the first part of the week. The last half was mostly partly cloudy and cool.

Corn and sorghums are making rapid growth. The corn was cultivated for the third time during the week, and the second cutting of alfalfa is being put up. Soil sampling during the week indicated that there is from 3 to 4 feet of moisture in the fallow plots and some moisture in the first foot in the stubble plots. Small plots of bromegrass and crested wheatgrass were harvested and will be used to reseed the sod plots. The sorghum plots were thinned and the potatoes sprayed and cultivated.

O. R. Mathews visited the station on Tuesday.

Maximum temperature, 105°; minimum, 65°; precipitation, none.

AKRON:

The protracted dry, hot period was broken, at least temporarily, by an inch of rain Wednesday night. This storm, after the first burst, settled down into a nice drizzle which extended well into the night. It has been appreciably cooler since.

Harvesting was practically completed and threshing might have been started by Friday afternoon had the bundle grain been dry enough. The straw yield on fallow preparations will be heavy.

Grasshoppers concentrating on the corn plots damaged some
of this crop appreciably. Poisoned bait was scattered on two
occasions this past week in a further effort to diminish their
numbers. Blister beetles made their annual appearance and
practically skeletonized the recently emerged potato plants before
control measures could be brought into play.

O. R. Mathews of the Division Staff visited Monday.

Maximum temperature, 101°; minimum, 57°; precipitation, 1.00 inch.

COLBY:

This has been a week of winds, dust, soil blowing, and hard
rains. A regular gully washer last Sunday afternoon smoothed the
surface of all fallow ground so that it blew very readily. Several
windy days followed, so that we have had an unusual amount of soil
blowing for July. Two showers since were not as hard. Considerable
of the water from Sunday's rain was lost by run-off, so there was
much washing, and all the lagoons were full. The Sunday rain
did not cover much territory and was heaviest at Colby.

The mid July seed-bed preparation for winter wheat was done
yesterday and today. The soil was in almost ideal condition for
working, although dry dirt was turned up in places. The sorghums
were cultivated for the first time and the corn was laid by. There
were almost no weeds, but the surface was smooth and rather hard.
The sorghums are from 4 to 12 inches high, the corn from 30 to
36 inches. The fallows were also worked to break the crust so as
to make it more receptive to water and to keep it from blowing.
There were almost no weeds on the fallow plots. A very hard shower
fell this afternoon after the fallow plots had been worked and
smoothed the surface down again for the most part.

Wheat yields are ranging from almost nothing to better
than 30 bushels to the acre in this county. The average will be
under 10 bushels. The late wheat was all very poor. The test
ranges from less than 50 pounds to as high as 64 pounds to the
bushel. With the farm price at less than 60 cents many fields
did not pay the expenses of cutting, which was generally about
a dollar per acre and 5 cents per bushel for combining.

Maximum temperature, 107°; minimum, 59°; precipitation, 1.96 inches.

HAYS:

The weather during the first half of the week for most part
was clear and hot. The last two days have been cloudy and cooler.

Except for the plants that have been mutilated by grasshoppers,
the corn is making good growth. It seems the grasshoppers are
determined to destroy most of the corn. Kafir and milo crops
are making good growth, and thus far these crops are not suffering
from the grasshoppers.

Combine thrashing was finished Monday, and shock thrashing
of barley, oats, spring wheat, and a few plots of winter wheat was
finished Thursday. Corn was cultivated Friday and sorghums are
being cultivated today. Soil samples for moisture determinations
are being taken on plots on which seedbed preparation for wheat will
be started Monday.

The ground is very dry and hard on the small grain plots and is turning very cloddy. A good rain would improve conditions generally.

Maximum temperature, 109°; minimum, 66°; precipitation, 0.02 inch.

GARDEN CITY:

A 0.79 inch rain fell this week, but it was quite local. Considerably more rain was received a few miles northeast of the station. Dust blew in on one day, but it was not severe. Temperatures remained rather high the first part of the week, for there were 5 consecutive days of 101° or above maximums.

Field work consisted of cultivating row crops, hoeing weeds, and taking soil moisture samples. Five plots of wheat on fallow were combined. They were the only plots which had sufficient wheat to get yields on.

Grasshoppers are still very numerous and a dozer will be constructed to aid in controlling them.

Station visitors were C. O. Grandfield, Assistant Agronomist U.S.D.A., and A. L. Clapp, in charge of cooperative experiments, both of Kansas State College.

Maximum temperature, 105°; minimum, 64°; precipitation, 0.79 inch.

TUCUMCARI:

Cool, cloudy weather the latter part of the week revived young row crops, which were rolling and in dire need of rain early in the week. Ranges are browning fast. Rains in several directions have been reported, but 0.01 inch received this week is the local total for the month to date. In June 1.49 inches was received. The total for the year, 6.42 inches, is some 2 inches below the normal for the period.

Thinning of plots is nearly completed; practically all plot and increase land was either cultivated or knifed during the week. Station crops are clean and in condition to make excellent growth if rain occurs.

Some 80 local Kiwanians and Rotarians had lunch at the station Thursday, touring the station prior to lunch.

Maximum temperature, 101°; minimum, 61°; wind velocity, 6.4 miles per hour.

DALHART:

As it continued dry during the week, the prospects are still anything but encouraging for producing a crop this season. The sorghums have now reached that stage where the moisture shortage is resulting in stunted growth. The height is extremely variable at which the growth is arrested, ranging from 2 to 10 inches. A few plots continue near-normal growth. It was necessary to cultivate some more dry plots where the 'goat-head' weeds were especially troublesome. Other work consisted of thinning rotation plots (there still remains about a week of this thinning because of the lateness of planting), soil moisture sampling, and hoeing of the conifer spacing test.

Survival counts were made on the conifer planting. The planting was originally made in 1932, and replacements have been made annually since, excepting 1935. The entire planting at the start consisted of 2784 trees distributed among 5 species. A brief summary is given here for one species, redcedar, in the planting. At the start of the 1938 planting season 80 percent of a perfect stand had been secured for redcedars. The remaining 20 percent were filled in in the spring of 1938. By May 1 with the exception of a few doubtful trees this species showed 100 percent stand. On July 15 only 70 percent were alive. At the start of 1938 26 percent of the perfect stand were of trees planted in 1932; 60 percent of the 1932 trees have died since spring of this year, so that less than 11 percent of the planting of redcedars is now of the 1932 setting. Other years for the planting show a higher survival and about the same percentage of survival ranging from 78 to 85 percent survival of those trees alive at the start of growth in 1938. The high death loss was in the more vigorous and larger trees. The continued and prolonged drought is the reason why the larger trees have dried out and died.

Maximum temperature, 101°; minimum, 63°; precipitation, 0.07 inch in two rains; precipitation January 1 - July 15, 4.45 inches; normal 9.51 inches.

BIG SPRING:

Maximum temperatures during the week have remained constantly hot, the maximum stopping around 100° each day. While this temperature is not high, low wind velocity makes it rather oppressive.

Cotton and all feedstuffs have continued to make a rapid growth during the week. Some of the early varieties of sorghums in the May 15 date of planting are starting to head. It is very doubtful if comparable yields can be obtained from this date of planting, as the sand and washing rains cut some of the varieties to very thin stands.

Thinning some increase milo, hoeing scattered weeds from all plots, and cultivating occupied most of the time of the force. A late planting of two early sorghum varieties, Early kalo and Sooner milo was made July 15; pinto beans was also planted on this date.

Maximum temperature, 100°; minimum, 68°; precipitation, none.

WOODWARD:

Cloudy weather with strong threats of rain has prevailed for the last 3 days, the result being 0.11 inch distributed over the 3-day period. The cool, cloudy weather was a big help to the corn. The dry, warm winds from the south were drying the tassels and silks too fast until checked by the damp, cool period. The sky has cleared now (Saturday, 3 p.m.) and the wind is blowing as though the tide had changed, without a beneficial rain, to dry, warm weather again.

Row crops are making rapid growth. Replanted plots of kafir and milo and contour basin listed plots of kafir and milo were thrown in with the lister cultivator. Cotton on the west place has began to bloom and yet cotton on the east place which was replanted is as large, but no blooms have set on. Soil difference is probably the chief reason for the size of plants and age of plants to setting on of blooms.

Work consisted of threshing fertilizer wheat plots, seeding sewed-feed plot, mowing weeds on clover, lespedeza, and alfilaria plots, cultivating field wheat and row crops, hauling two cars of pipe and two cars of fence posts from the depot to the station, taking soil samples, and relisting and damming fallow plots.

Visitors were Dr. H. G. Gernert, Okla. A & M College, Stillwater; and Dr. Geib, Soil Conservation Service, College Station, Texas.

Maximum temperature, 103°; minimum, 68°; precipitation, 0.11 inch.

NOTE:

D. E. Stephens, senior agronomist in the Division of Cereal Crops and Diseases, and superintendent of the Sherman Branch Experiment Station at Mere, Oregon, since 1912 has been appointed principal agronomist in the Soil Conservation Service effective July 1, 1938. His headquarters are being transferred to Washington, D. C., where he will act as a coordinator between the Soil Conservation Service and the Bureau of Plant Industry. Cereal Courier, July 10, 1938.

Fay A. Wagner, superintendent of the Garden City Branch Station, resigned effective June 30. L. M. Sloan, formerly county agent at Garden City and for the last three years with the Soil Conservation Service, has been appointed to the position.

Technical Bulletin 617, "Conservation and Use of Soil Moisture at Mandan, N. Dak.", by J. C. Thysell has been received from the printer. Franks have been furnished for a limited number to be sent to each station.

O. R. Mathews returned to Washington July 21.

--ooOoo--

WEEKLY STATION REPORTS

OF THE DIVISION OF

DRY LAND AGRICULTURE

BUREAU OF PLANT INDUSTRY

U. S. DEPARTMENT OF AGRICULTURE

GPO   123668

REPORT FOR THE WEEK ENDING JULY 23, 1938.

HAVRE:

The past week was the warmest of the season, with a maximum of 97°. There was only a trace of precipitation, skies were mostly clear, and wind movement continued relatively light.

Small grains ripened rapidly in the experimental field, harvest of barley, oats, and winter wheat being started generally. Grain hays were mowed, cured, and weighed, yields of oats and spring rye on fallow exceeding 2 tons of field cured forage per acre. With warmer weather, corn is making excellent progress, considerable crossing and inbreeding having been done in the corn nursery.

The farm department was engaged in harvesting spring rye for hay, binding an increase seed field of crested wheatgrass, and cutting prairie hay for horses. Blister beetles, now numerous, may injure the second crop of alfalfa to some extent. Grasshoppers as yet are not very prevalent.

Visitors included E. J. George of the Mandan Field Station; J. Allen Clark, of the Cereal Division; J. G. Diamond, Montana Crop Reporting Service; E. B. Duncan, Great Northern Agricultural Agent; V. H. Florell and party of SCS; and H. V. Mills, Entomologist, Mentana Experiment Station. A 4-H Club camp of some 250 members under the direction of R. E. Cameron, State Club Leader occupied the barracks building.

Maximum temperature, 97°; minimum, 51°; precipitation, 0.02 inch.

JUDITH BASIN:

Five of the past seven days had temperatures of 80° or more. The dry, hot winds are ripening and drying crops rapidly. Cutting of small grains will commence during the coming week, unless moisture is soon received.

The biggest part of the week was spent in making preparations for the Association's 29th Annual Judith Basin Picnic which was held on Thursday. Although many farmers were busy haying, some 267 cars were admitted which was 21 more than last year. Senator B. K. Wheeler and President Strand of the Montana State College headed the speaking program.

J. Allen Clark, Cereal Crops and Diseases, was an official visitor during the week.

Maximum temperature, 92°; minimum, 49°; precipitation, 0.05 inch.

HUNTLEY:

Warm, dry weather throughout the week has been excellent for maturing small grains. Binder harvesting is well under way, and a few early fields of winter wheat have been cut with combines. The bulk of the combine harvesting on the larger wheat ranches will not start until next week, however. Yield reports from local fields harvested during the week have ranged from 18 to 26 bushels to the acre of winter wheat. The quality of the grain is high.

Cutting of winter wheat, oats, and barley has been completed on the plots. Spring wheat is turning rapidly and should be ready for the binder in a few days. The more mature plots of crested wheatgrass were also harvested. Mowing of alfalfa for the second time this season is under way today.

Additional field work has consisted of hoeing corn and other row crops, duckfooting fallow, and clipping spring-sown alfalfa.

Maximum temperature, 96°; minimum, 47°; precipitation, 0.01 inch.

SHERIDAN:

Following heavy showers on the 16th, moderate weather prevailed over the remainder of the week, with only a trace of precipitation and only one day with a temperature of 90° or above. Grain continued to ripen, and harvesting was continued over the first two days of the week and again the last two days. The remainder of the second growth alfalfa, which was mostly light, was cut. Sheep were weighed and the pastures changed. Growth of late crops continues excellent.

J. Allen Clark was at the station the 21st to go over the spring wheat varieties.

Maximum temperature, 92°; minimum, 47°; precipitation, 1.32 inches.

DICKINSON:

Dry weather with moderate temperature was favorable for harvesting and haying. Garden crops, corn, and late forage crops would be benefitted by rain.

Grasshoppers are still very numerous and are still damaging nearly all vegetation. So far there is little apparent damage to native grass, but hoppers are numerous in all grassland and are living on something. The greatest movement into the locality was on July 10, and so far there has been no great decrease in numbers. Poison bait has been scattered about the station, and some spraying and continuous dusting has given some protection to the garden crops.

Wheat on the rotations was cut July 18 and 19 because of damage by grasshoppers. Wheat varieties have nearly all been cut, and most of the cereal nursery has been harvested, all having been cut well on the green side to try to save something from the grasshoppers. Many farmers in the district will not harvest any wheat, as nearly all of the heads have been cut off by the hoppers. That which is left by the hoppers is greener and badly damaged by rust. Corn still has a chance to make a good crop if the hoppers should thin out. So far only occasional plants have been cut off and some of the leaves have been damaged.

Crested wheatgrass is being harvested a little on the green side. So far the hoppers have not greatly damaged the heads in larger fields, but the leaves were eaten about two weeks ago. Yields apparently will be average or better. Most of the seed has been cut from bromegrass plots.

Hay is being cut from native grassland in the district. Blue grama grass, the most important constituent of this hay, has made an outstanding growth and is apparently maturing the best seed crop in many years.

Visitors included T. R. Stanton and J. A. Clark, Cereal Crops and Diseases; E. G. Davis, Bureau of Entomology; and E. C. Johnson, Executive Secretary Billings County Welfare Board, Medora, N. Dak.

Maximum temperature, 89°; minimum, 46°; precipitation, 0.03 inch.

MANDAN:

Agronomy - The past week remained dry and fairly cool.

Crested wheatgrass was harvested for seed, and most of the grain varieties and barley in the rotations were harvested. Harvesting will be general on the station next week.

Grasshoppers are fairly thick, but so far damage has not been serious.

Maximum temperature, 91°; minimum, 53°; precipitation, 0.05 inch.

Cooperative Grazing Experiment - Vegetation on the prairie is starting to dry up. Blue grama grass is showing the effects of drought. The volume of growth of this grass is the best for a number of years. It is heavily headed out all over the country and gives premise of the best seed crop since 1928.

Horticulture - The weather has been dry during the week, and a good rain would now be beneficial. However, horticultural trees and shrubs are continuing to make a good growth.

Weeds, especially purslane, continue to flourish, and cultivating and hoeing have been in progress.

Gooseberries are being picked. Yields in the coulee were much higher than in the regular variety test. Carry is one of the highest yielding varieties. Golden currants and sandcherries will be picked next week.

Vegetables continue to yield well and so far do not seem to be much affected by lack of water.

Tomatoes are beginning to ripen in the acre garden, where the pruning and staking method is in effect. In the variety test, the Redskin is demonstrating its extreme earliness and heavy yielding qualities. It is lacking in size but the other qualities make up for it.

Sweet corn breeding has been in progress all week. With but a few exceptions, all selections this year seem very good so far as uniformity and freedom from disease is concerned.

The lawns having shown indications of need of water, are being irrigated at the present time.

Arboriculture - E. J. George, inspecting cooperative shelterbelts in Montana, writes as follows:

"Havre, July 16. Grasshoppers are moving west, though not reached this vicinity in large numbers yet. Other insects are apparently causing damage to grain in this locality."

"Shelby, July 19. Sugarbeet webworms extremely bad in this locality, damaging gardens severely and stripping other vegetation. Grain good."

Among the visitors at the station during the week were H. R. Sumner with some 20 elevator managers and seedsmen; T. R. Stanton, Cereal Crops and Diseases; J. E. Pallesen (Manhattan, Kans.) and A. J. King (Agric. Stat., Washington, D.C.) Division of Crop and Livestock Estimates.

BELLE FOURCHE:

With the exception of one hot day, moderate temperatures favorable to crop development prevailed throughout the week. Light rains were received on July 19 and 20, but they were of little value to vegetation. Corn is withstanding the continued dry weather remarkably well and is beginning to tassel. Sudan grass and sorgo are making very rapid growth, but potatoes have made no appreciable recovery from grasshopper damage.

Grasshoppers are much less numerous on the dry land rotation field than in previous weeks. This is partly due to exceptionally heavy kills obtained from recent distributions of poison bait, and to possible migrations away from the field. Corn and potatoes now appear to have a chance of surviving and producing yields if rain is received.

J. A. Clark, Cereal Crops and Diseases, visited the station on July 22.

Maximum temperature, 94°; minimum, 52°; precipitation, 0.19 inch.

ARCHER:

The weather during the week ending July 23 was rather cool. Precipitation was recorded during the first five days of the week, the total being 1.01 inches. This, in addition to the 0.42 inch received during the latter part of the week ending July 16, soaked into the soil and but little run-off occurred. Local showers were prevalent. In sections where no rains occurred the crops are burning badly.

At the station the winter wheat is ripening, the barley is ripe, and the winter rye has been harvested. Corn is beginning to tassel, and millet gives good prospects of a large hay crop. The rains improved the prospects of potatoes and beans. At lower altitudes the winter wheat harvest is progressing rapidly.

Station work consisted of cultivating the corn in the dairy field, hauling spring wheat hay, hoeing, and preparing for the annual Field Day which was held July 20.

In addition to the station's implements the John Deere Company, International Harvester Company, and the Wortham Machinery Company furnished demonstration machinery for Field Day.

Prominent Field Day visitors were Wallace Bond, President of the Board of Trustees of the University of Wyoming; A. J. King, President of the Wyoming State Farm Bureau; Director W. L. Quayle, University of Wyoming; Wilkie Collins and Dick Llewellyn, Soil Conservation Service; and A.W.Krofchek,Forester of the Cheyenne Horticultural Field Station.

Maximum temperature, 82°; minimum, 48°; precipitation,1.01 inches.

NORTH PLATTE:

Temperatures of less than 90° prevailed throughout most of the week. No rain has been recorded during the past 17 days. The corn is silking and still looks good. Moisture can be found to a depth of 3 feet in the corn plats, but rain will be needed soon to prevent injury to this crop. Grasshoppers are damaging silks as they emerge from the ear shoot. The sorghums are looking good, and the early varieties seeded May 23 are heading. Pastures are drying up and show the effects of the drought. No moisture is in evidence in the sod land.

Threshing began this week. Winter wheat yields range from 6 to 36 bushels. The methods of fallow plats averaged about 30 bushels per acre of 57' to 60 pounds per bushel. The wheat on plats after wheat is shriveled, weighing about 50 pounds per bushel. All wheat except that in thin stands is poor in color.

Dr. Quisenberry visited the station Thursday and Friday to supervise the nursery threshing. Dean W. W. Burr of the College of Agriculture at Lincoln, also spent a few days at the station.

Maximum temperature, 99°; minimum, 57°; precipitation, none.

AKRON:

Showers and some hail about the general region caused the week's weather to remain cool. Station crops are holding nicely on the 1 inch of rainfall received the 13th. Corn is beginning to tassel, and early proso varieties are coming into head. Dry beans were thinned to specified stands for a rate of seeding test. A nursery and an outside threshing crew were busy all week. Rotation plots were cleared, and a start was made on the cereal varieties by the week end.

Average yields in the rotations were barley, 24.2 bushels; oats, 28.7 bushels; spring wheat, 5.8 bushels; and winter wheat, 12.2 bushels.

The barley and oat yields are above average while those of the spring and winter wheat are about average.

Rotation fallow plots and the cereal variety fallow were leveled by means of the rod weeder this week end. This machine does a nice job of weeding on the station hard land following the use of the peacock damming lister.

Glen Kinghorn and T. G. Stewart, State extension staff, visited Tuesday. K. S. Quisenberry and J. J. Curtis met here Wednesday in the interest of cereal small grain investigational work.

COLBY:

The rainy weather continued the first half of this week. Threatening clouds have come up every day, but the last three days have been rainless with practically no wind. The temperatures have been cool, making it almost ideal for field work. The frequent showers earlier in the week delayed the completion of harvest, so that combines are still seen here and there.

Corn and the sorghums have made very rapid growth and now appear very promising. There is very little corn left in the locality as grasshoppers have destroyed a large part of the small acreage planted. That which is left is beginning to tassel. Grasshoppers are still numerous and may work on the tassels and silks to a very damaging extent.

Maximum temperature, 90°; minimum, 56°; precipitation, 1.36 inches.

HAYS:

The weather has been partly cloudy with warm days and cool nights. Three light showers have occurred, but the ground is dry and feed crops are beginning to need moisture, especially the drilled feed crops which are now wilting. Pastures are turning brown.

The initial tillage work for all early seedbed preparation is finished. The entire week has been spent on tillage and soil moisture determinations. All stubble land is dry and turns up cloddy.

S. D. Flora, Meteoriologist, Topeka, Kans., was a visitor at the station Monday.

Maximum temperature, 96°; minimum, 59°; precipitation, 0.62 inch.

LAWTON:

Four light showers fell this week, which totaled 0.23 inch. They benefited only by holding down the temperatures. A mild dust storm blew in from the northeast on one day, but it lasted only a few minutes.

Row crops are doing well in most cases, but a few are showing signs of lack of moisture. A grasshopper dozer has been constructed which is fastened to the front bumper of the pickup truck. This is being used on Sudan grass and alfalfa plots with very good results.

Field work consisted of early fall tillage work, hoeing weeds, and taking soil moisture samples.

Maximum temperature, 94°; minimum, 59°; precipitation, 0.23 inch.

TUCUMCARI:
     Three showers early in the week, totaling 0.98 inch,
revived crops and ranges but prevented field work until
yesterday. Late planted crops, plots and increase, have
emerged to good stands.
     Total precipitation for the year to date, 7.40 inches,
is 1.5 inches below normal for the period, but ranges and
crops are in better than normal condition. Temperatures have
been low, with much cloudy weather, and evaporation and wind
movement have been exceptionally low. Normal precipitation
throughout the balance of the growing season should produce
good yields of row crops.
     Full grown migratory grasshoppers have appeared the
past 2 days from the northeast. It has not been learned as yet
whether they will prove a crop hazard.
     E. W. Johnson and the New Mexico extension service
horticulturist spent the early portion of the week in this
locality.
     Maximum temperature, 96°; minimum, 58°.

DALHART:
     Local showers during the past week have given opportunity
to plant the late planting of the grain sorghums and to
complete planting for forage and for soil protection. This
planting has occupied so much of the time that 'goatheads' on
the early planting have grown to the extent that eradication
of them will be no small job. The thinning of all of the
earlier planted material was completed during the week. `For
the first time this spring it was possible to cultivate the
vineyard and tree plantings while the ground was moist. Four
local showers were received during the week. While they covered
the station fairly uniformly, the soil less than a mile south
of the station remains dry.
     Maximum temperature, 95°;minimum, 58°;precipitation,1.30 inches.

BIG SPRING:
     During the past week no field work was accomplished, as
rains varying in amounts from 0.08 to 1.27 inches were received
on each of five days. The total for this period is 2.97 inches
with rain still falling at this writing. All crops present a
rich, deep, green color and are growing rapidly.
     Some parts of the county are reporting some leaf worm
damage to the cotton, and this week of cloudy, wet weather will
provide good conditions for the worm infestation to spread.
     Maximum temperature, 99°;minimum, 65°;precipitation,2.97 inches.

LAWTON:

Very moderate temperatures since   July 14 have been highly beneficial to sorghums and cotton that have been blooming with only scant supplies of moisture. Unsettled weather has prevailed, and a few good showers have been reported in various localities. In the immediate vicinity of Lawton, the July rainfall has been negligible.

Kafir and feterita in the rotation plots have been fully headed since July 15. These plots carry a very heavy infestation of chinch bugs and the basal foliage is badly fired. Additional moisture in the near future will be necessary to avoid premature ripening of the grain.

Cotton blooms are gradually increasing to a peak bloom period, and but few squares have been shed so far. Plant growth is still somewhat less than normal.

Stubble land is too hard and dry to permit any tillage at present. Plot plowing, disking, and listing was completed July 12, leaving the ground in a very rough, lumpy condition.

Maximum temperatures from the 13th to the 24th ranged from 86 to 99.

WOODWARD:

Most of the week was cool and cloudy. Temperatures reached 90° on three days with the remainder down in the 80's. The maximum temperature was 94° on July 17 and minimum 62° on the 22nd. Three showers were received: 1.01 inches on Saturday night, 0.28 inch on Wednesday night, and 0.01 inch on Thursday. The rain on Wednesday night came from the south and reached only part of the station. Cultivation was continued the following morning on the northwest corner, but the south part was too wet to enter until the following day.

All row crops are growing very vigorously. Manured plots of sorghums have a darker green color and more growth than unmanured plots. Sorghums seeded in basin-listed seedbeds appear to be slower getting started than on other seedbed preparations.

Tomatoes are ripening rapidly. A small amount of tomato hybridizing has been done. Young grape vines have been sprouted and trained up.

Construction on the dam has begun. Trees have been grubbed out and moving of dirt is under way but only on a small scale as yet.

Work consists of: listing roadways and one-waying between on the new addition, cleaning plot wheat, cultivating fallow plots, trimming plots, cultivating field sorghums, and hauling two carloads of posts from the depot to the station.

---ooooo0OOo0ooooo---

WEEKLY STATION REPORTS

OF THE DIVISION OF

DRY LAND AGRICULTURE

BUREAU OF PLANT INDUSTRY

U. S. DEPARTMENT OF AGRICULTURE

GPO   123668

REPORT FOR THE WEEK ENDING JULY 30, 1938

HAVRE:

Cool showery weather early in the week delayed field work for two days, followed by clearing skies and somewhat higher temperatures.

Small grain projects harvested in the experimental field included winter wheat, barley, and most of the oats in the D.L.A. section; oats, barley, and winter wheat nurseries; winter wheat and barley varieties; all dates of seeding winter wheat; and other miscellaneous plantings. Corn continued to make excellent progress; and flax is rapidly maturing.

The general farm department has about completed harvesting the grain hay crop, a very heavy forage yield of oats and spring rye being obtained, as indicated by the use of nearly 3.5 pounds of binder twine per acre.

Among numerous station visitors were W. T. Pecora, Harvard geologist; F. A. Coffman and R. H. Bamberg of the Cereal Division; L. P. Reitz, Forage Crops; and R. D. Mercer, Extension Agronomist.

Maximum temperature, 90°; minimum, 52°; precipitation, 0.91 inch.

JUDITH BASIN:

This week opened with three days of light precipitation, the remainder of the week was dry and of moderate temperatures.

Harvesting was begun with the cutting of many of the rotation oats and winter wheat, winter wheat tillage belts, one block of crested wheatgrass for seed, and small grains for hay.

Haying should be completed this coming week, provided the cutting of small grains do not demand too much time.

Visitors include E. J. George, Mandan; and Dr. R. H. Bamberg, Bozeman.

Maximum temperature, 85°; minimum, 47°; precipitation, 0.24 inch.

HUNTLEY:

Climatic conditions throughout the week were beneficial to crop development. Precipitation occurred almost daily, but with one exception the showers were light and did not interfere with work in the fields. Shocked grains and haycocks had to be opened up for drying early in the week following a rain of 0.54 inch, much of which was torrential in character. Combine harvesting of winter wheat on neighboring ranches was delayed until the last of the week on account of showers. Yields from the later grains are much higher than from those harvested a week ago, 35 to 50 bushels to the acre now being reported.

Small-grain harvest was completed on the plots during the week, and the last of the second crop alfalfa was hauled in. The hay was of poor quality, due to weeds which came up thickly with the new crop. Crested wheatgrass is making a new growth on 30 acres of station pasture land that was swept by a grass fire a week ago.

Maximum temperature, 93°; minimum, 54°; precipitation, 0.65 inch.

SHERIDAN:

Temperatures continued slightly below the average for the season, with several sprinkles of rain, but no precipitation of consequence. In spite of moderate temperatures, however, grain ripened rapidly. Harvesting of small grain on the station, with the exception of late dates of seeding and a few late maturing plots in the varieties of oats and spring wheat, was completed Friday.

The station Field Day was held on the 28th. There was a good attendance, and apparently an increased interest in the results of the station work over that of previous years. W. L. Quayle, Director of State Farms, was a station visitor over the 27th and 28th and made the principal talk at the meeting.

Psyllid yellows or purple top was noted on potatoes and tomatoes early in the week. The crops were sprayed with lime-sulphur, but with only a low pressure sprayer available for the work, any benefit from the spraying appears doubtful. The disease apparently is wide spread over nearly all potato fields of the county.

Maximum temperature, 93°; minimum, 51°; precipitation, 0.07 inch.

DICKINSON:

During the heat on Saturday July 23 when the temperature reached 96°, the maximum of the year to date, there was an active movement of hoppers and they definitely thinned out. Enough remain to continue damage to late crops and to lay large numbers of eggs, if conditions remain favorable for long.

A shower of 0.35 inch on July 26 delayed harvest only a short time and was of benefit to corn and other late crops. Hoppers continued to work on corn, but some fields have been damaged little to date.

Harvesting of crested wheatgrass plots and increase blocks was completed. Durum wheat plots on field N were cut. This wheat was damaged less by grasshoppers than the common wheat on the rotations.

Fallow plots on the main field were cultivated, and miscellaneous cultivation and weeding was finished.

Visitors included Messrs. Whitman, Jacobson, Hanson, and Sogstad, Dept. of Botany, N.D.A.C.

Maximum temperature, 96°; minimum, 46°; precipitation, 0.35 inch. Precipitation, July, 3.12 inches.

MANDAN:

Agronomy: Harvest was delayed two days during the week because of rain, which was recorded on three days and was of benefit to corn, as the crop was nearing the wilting point.

All grain plots were harvested in the rotations. Grasshoppers had cut off some grain heads, but the damage was not serious. More damage had been done in the feed fields. Harvest of the feed field is in progress.

Maximum temperature, 97°; minimum, 52°; precipitation, 1.40 inches.

Cooperative Grazing Experiment: Rains helped the blue grama grass, which was starting to dry up. It will likely now be able to set a heavy seed crop. Grama over the prairie is headed the heaviest in a number of years.

Horticulture: Sandcherries and Golden currants are being harvested. For the first time, birds have been numerous enough to consume a large part of the fruit. They seem to have a special liking for the sandcherries. Selections 24-38, 24-36, and 25-3 again look good and are a decided improvement over their parent, Sioux.

Weeds are again growing rapidly since the last rain, and another complete cultivation followed by hoeing is in order. Weeds on the hillside orchard terraces have been mowed.

Vegetables continue to mature and records of yields are taken daily. On the whole the different crops are very good. Peas are now almost through, but beans, cabbage, and tomatoes are now at their best. Early corn is maturing but is very badly infested with smut.

A very interesting test of the latest creations in tomato varieties is now in evidence. The two latest varieties introduced by the North Dakota Agricultural College are by far the earliest and most prolific, but also seem more acid than any other tomatoes.

The lawns were beginning to show evidence of drought and were irrigated during the week.

Platycodon, Gaillardia and Hemerocalli are at present at their best and show up very well in perennial beds and borders. Hybrid rugosa roses have been in bloom since spring and are still producing a fine show of blossoms.

Arboriculture: E. J. George is expected back tonight or Sunday and will remain a few days at the Field Station before continuing the inspection of cooperative shelterbelts.

Visitors for the week included A. C. Dillman, Cereal Crops and Diseases; M. R. Lewis and Leslie Bowen, Bureau of Agricultural Economics, Division of Irrigation. Dr. C. E. Leighty arrived at the Field Station on Friday.

BELLE FOURCHE:

A strong hot wind on July 23 was very injurious to corn, and the leaves remained permanently curled afterwards, although the following three days were cool and cloudy, and 0.54 inch precipitation was received on July 25. Sudan grass and sorgo are beginning to head, but the drought apparently is commencing to check the growth of these crops.

Only 1.13 inches precipitation were recorded in July, as compared with the average of 2.39 inches for the month. The total precipitation for the year to date is 7.41 inches, which is 3.61 inches below normal.

Daily migrations of grasshoppers during the latter part of the week have again increased the number of pests present on the dry land rotation field to alarming proportions, and extensive damage is being done to corn and potatoes.

Threshing of all crops, except flax, was completed. The highest, lowest, and average yields obtained were as follows:

Yield per acre

	Highest		Lowest		Average all plots
W. Rye	13.2 bus.,	(Rot. 412)	8.9 bus.,	(Rot. 410)	10.5 bus.
W. Wheat	25.7 "	(CC-C)	6.7 "	(" 409)	14.5 "
S. Wheat	18.8 "	(Rot. 15)	1.2 "	(" 42)	7.8 "
Oats	28.1 "	(CC-C)	0 "	(" 10, 41, 42)	9.9 "
Barley	34.0 "	(CC-C)	5.2 "	(" 7)	16.3 "

Maximum temperature, 97°; minimum, 52°; precipitation, 0.54 inch.

ARCHER:
Precipitation was recorded during five days. Two showers of 0.18 and 0.20 inch occurred July 25 and 28, respectively. To date the total precipitation during July is 2.12 inches, which is 0.23 of an inch more than the 25-year average.

Small grains are maturing rapidly. At the station the barley, winter wheat, and early seeded spring wheat have been harvested and threshing preparations are underway. Corn is sending out its first tassel shoots. Purple top has greatly reduced the prospects of a good potato crop. Beans are doing well. The summer weather has been too cool for the sorghum crop. Millet has made a good growth but is in need of rain. The grasses have held up well.

Maximum temperature, 90°; minimum, 50°; precipitation, 0.40 inch.

NORTH PLATTE:
Three light showers fell during the week, which interrupted threshing operations. Cool weather prevailed throughout the week. The month's precipitation totaled 2.99 inches or 0.33 inch above normal. All the rain except that which fell this week came in two heavy rains the first week of the month. The sorghums drilled on fallow are still looking good. Early seedings of early varieties of sorghum are fully headed, and the early ones seeded June 7 are beginning to head. The corn is fully tasseled.

Threshing of the grain on the D.L.A. plots was completed this week, and most of the early fall plowing is completed. The oats on cropped land averaged about 25 bushels per acre, while those after fallow averaged about 35 bushels. The barley yields ranged from 25 to 30 bushels.

Maximum temperature, 99°; minimum, 60°; precipitation, 0.69 inch.

Precipitation Jan. - July, Normal, 12.57 inches.
1938 ,15.20 inches.

AKRON:

Weather remained cool with local showers, the station receiving measurable amounts on 5 separate days. The only consequential rain during the month was the 1.00 inch received July 13. This marks the second consecutive month with precipitation considerably below normal.

Nursery threshing was completed about the middle of the week. Variety threshing will require about 10 more days to complete.

Grain sorghum stands in the variety experiment are very unsatisfactory, a condition that could not be corrected because of the lateness of the original planting. The 10 acre increase field of Highland kafir across the railroad does not promise over one third of a stand. Corn stands also are relatively thin, but this crop has not as yet suffered from the low rainfall of June and July. All fall crops are still in excellent condition to profit by rain.

E. A. Norton of Washington, Roy Hockensmith of Amarillo, and W. W. Pate of Rapid City, all S.C.S. Officials, stopped Saturday afternoon.

Maximum temperature, 93°; minimum, 53°; precipitation, 0.37 inch.

COLBY:

This vicinity was visited by two more good rains this week. The weather has been fairly cool, also, and there has not been much wind, except part of the time when it was raining. The rains have been fairly general, but were much heavier in some places than in others. The station seems to be getting its full share of the precipitation visiting this county. The rains have come rather fast and hard, and run-off has been rather heavy with considerable washing in bare fields. There is very little weed growth for the amount of moisture we have had.

Corn and the sorghums are making excellent growth. The corn is about tasseled, and the Colby milo is beginning to head. Grasshoppers are numerous but are not doing much damage at present. The stand of corn was thinned considerably by them earlier in the season, but what is left is not being hurt. The moisture is down about 2 feet on fallow and over 1 foot in stubble ground that was dry at harvest.

Maximum temperature, 98°; minimum, 61°; precipitation, 1.65 inches.

HAYS:

The temperatures during the week have been moderate for July, and the sky has been partly cloudy threatening rain at times, but no rain of value has occurred. The ground continues to get drier, and row crops are wilting during the heat of the day indicating more moisture is needed.

It appears that we are in a dry spot, good rains having been reported around us.

The work during the week has consisted largely of making up and spreading poison bait for grasshoppers, soil moisture determinations, making count of stand of row crops, and a small amount of tillage work.

Maximum temperature, 99°; minimum, 63°; precipitation, 0.20 inch.

GARDEN CITY:

Rainfall amounted to 0.43 inch, which aided in keeping down the temperature. The past few weeks has been rather cool for this time of the year, as there has not been a maximum over 98° since July 13.

Row crops are making fair growth, and there are no signs of burning as yet. Sorghums in general over this area are making good growth. Those under irrigation are receiving adequate water, as the ditches from the river are full.

Station visitors were F. C. Fenton, Head of Agriculture Engineering Department, Kansas State College, and Donald Christy, Assistant Professor in Agricultural Engineering, College Station, Texas.

Maximum temperature, 98°; minimum, 64°; precipitation, 0.43 inch.

TUCUMCARI:

No rain occurred the past week, ranges are browning, and row crops are in need of moisture. Total precipitation, year to date, 7.40 inches, is approximately 2 inches below normal for the period.

Wind movement has been low, temperatures normal. The season seems unusually cool, but only because the past few summers have had unusually high temperatures.

Completion of the early July plot thinning, considerable cultivating, bagging of heads, and note taking comprisod the week's work.

Maximum temperature, 96°; minimum, 61°.

DALHART:

It continued dry during the week. The early planted, (June 1) sorghums are hurt daily by a shortage of soil moisture. Other sorghums that have reached a height of from 10 to 16 inches are wilting badly for 6 to 7 hours during the day. While corn is showing more injury on early prepared land and is wilting on all plots, it is holding its green color remarkably well. First tasseling of corn was recorded to-day. Actually, during the past 4 or 5 days the crop prospects have deteriorated rapidly, except on thin or late planting. Material planted last week is hardly large enough to thin now. The rather uniform emergence of the rotation plots of cowpeas is striking. These were planted in soil too dry for emergence the last of June, and the full emergence occurred about a week ago.

Work during the week has consisted of cultivation of row plots and hoeing of 'goathead' weeds.

Maximum temperature, 94°; minimum, 59°; precipitation, 0.10 inch.

Precipitation, Jan. 1 to date, 5.85 inches.

BIG SPRING:

Some field work was finally accomplished during the later part of the week, after rain had held up operations during the first three days. During this time 2.27 inches was received, which ran the total for the month up to 5.35 inches. This is the highest rainfall recorded in July since 1902.

The ranges are as green as they normally are in the spring, and ranchers report that grass is better than it has been in many years. The cotton program this year caused the farmers to plant large acreages of Sudan grass, and with ample moisture during the past two months a rank growth has been obtained; now there is a brisk demand for cattle to graze it off.

Station crops are all making a rapid growth, but worms have riddled the leaves of milo and corn. Cotton leaf worms are showing up all to frequently, so it is probable that they will have to be poisoned during the coming week.

Dr. Whitfield of the Soil Conservation Service in Amarillo and Mr. Langley of the Spur Station visited here during the week.

Maximum temperature, 91°; minimum, 66°; precipitation, 2.27 inches.

WOODWARD:

Two showers: 0.77 inches on Thursday night and 0.01 on Friday, were welcomed. Sorghums were taking the moisture out very rapidly. The lower blades had begun turning brown on all sorghums planted June 10. Of the sorghums, broomcorn showed the effects of insufficient moisture the most. Over a period of two days (26th to 27th) broomcorn changed from a lush green to a light green. The only droughty effects apparent on others was on the lower leaves. Broomcorn is regaining the lush green color since the rain. An intensive lateral root development was noted when cultivating sorghums this week. Roots were picked up on outside shovels of cultivator in greater amounts than normally.

As a result of favorable moisture conditions, most range pastures in the locality are recovering fast from the effects of overgrazing and drought. Although much of the vegetation consisted of weeds and weedy-type grasses, the total forage has been ample for livestock, and many of the better species of grass are heading well and promise to produce a good seed crop.

Cultivating row crops, cleaning seed wheat, one-waying on new addition, disking north and south roadways, taking soil samples, and picking tomatoes constituted the majority of the work for the week.

Visitors for the week were: C. E. Fisher, Soil Conservation Service, Spur, Texas; and Messrs. Quinlan and Trumble, Soil Conservation Service, Perryton, Texas.

Maximum temperature, 100°; minimum, 65°; precipitation, 0.78 inch.

Lightning Source UK Ltd.
Milton Keynes UK
UKHW022345030119
334726UK00011B/1204/P

9 780331 378559